Jazz Styles
Level Two

Supplement to All Piano and Keyboard Methods

Compiled, Arranged and Edited by Wesley Schaum

Foreword

Jazz styles, evolving over many years, encompass a broad range including ragtime, blues, boogie, swing and rock. A casual, improvisational attitude is the common thread. The syncopated rhythms and harmonies have remained popular for many generations and provide fascinating educational material.

This collection of fun-to-learn solos teaches a variety of rhythms, key signatures, time signatures, phrase groups, touches and fingerings.

Index

SCHAUM PUBLICATIONS, INC.

10235 N. Port Washington Rd. • Mequon, WI 53092

www.schaumpiano.net

Entertainer

Scott Joplin

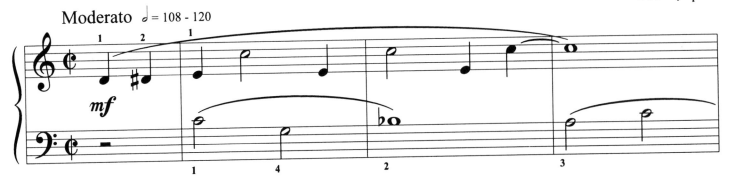

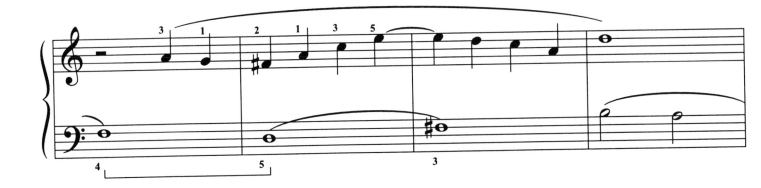

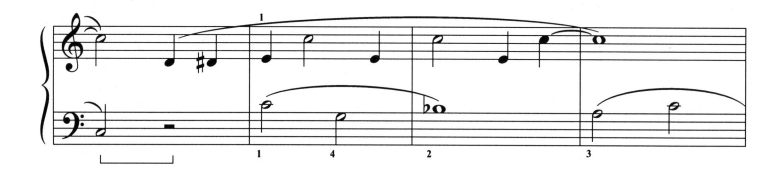

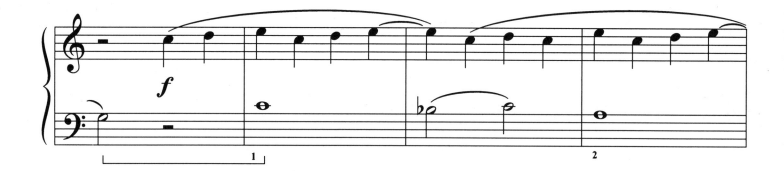

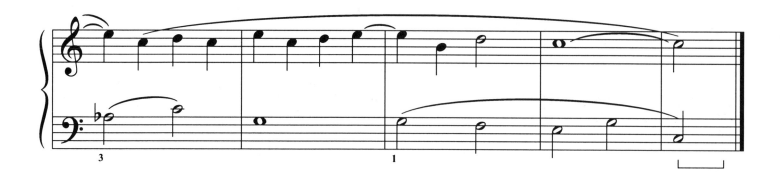

Sonic Boogie

Wesley Schaum

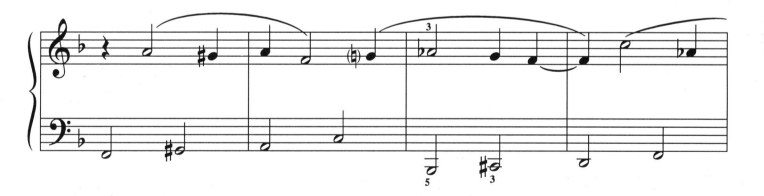

6

Cool School

Wesley Schaum

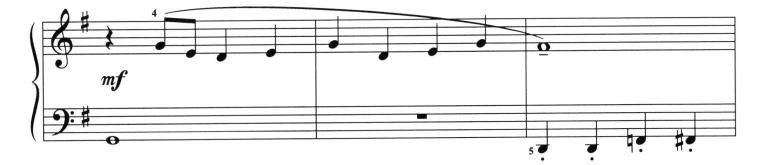

Rockin' Rhythm

Wesley Schaum

Big Beat

Wesley Schaum

Presto ♩ = 138 - 160

If desired, Swing 8th notes may be used:

Easy Come, Easy Go

Wesley Schaum

Allegro ♩= 126 - 144

Nappy Lee

Joe Jordan

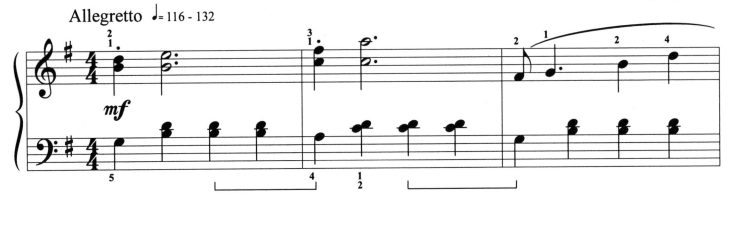

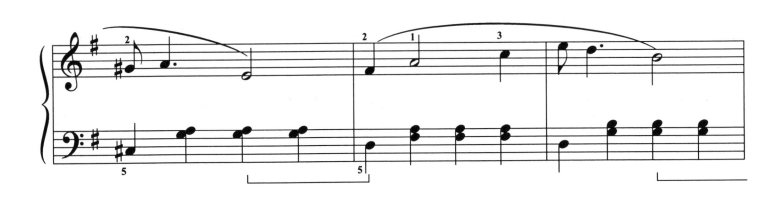

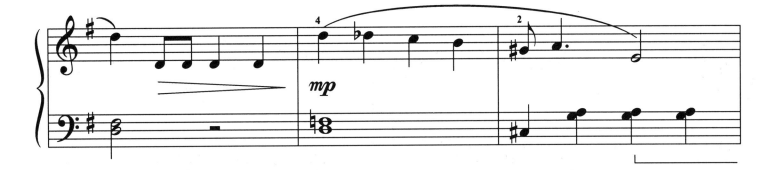

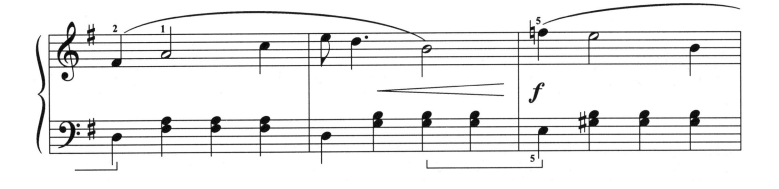

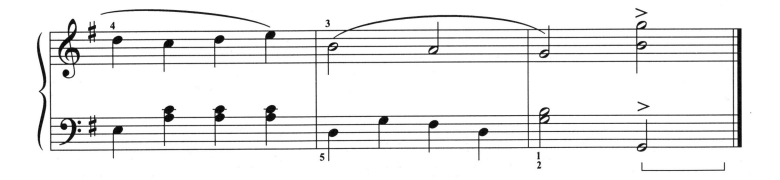

Baggy Boogie

Wesley Schaum

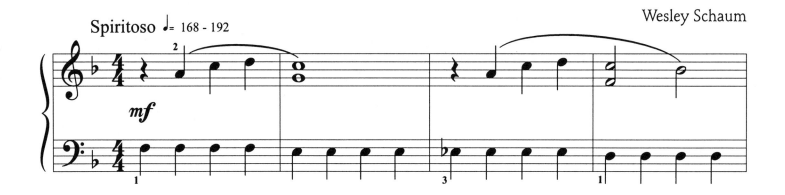

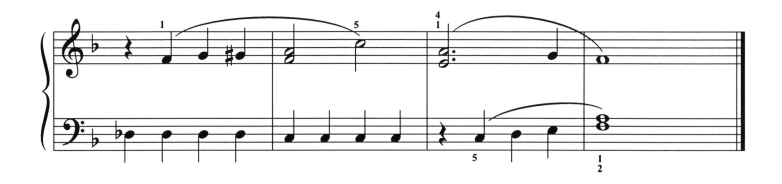

Ramblin' Rock

Wesley Schaum

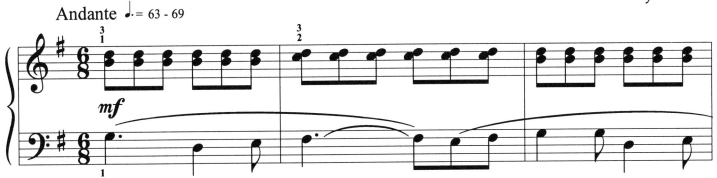

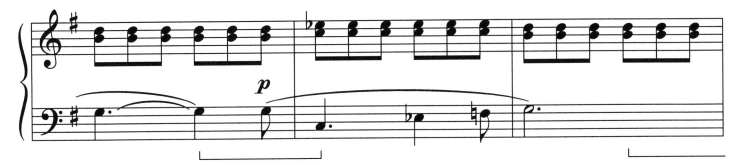

Surfin' Boogie

Wesley Schaum

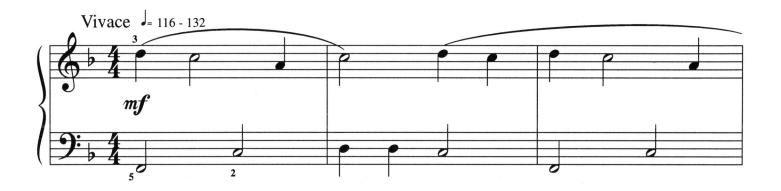

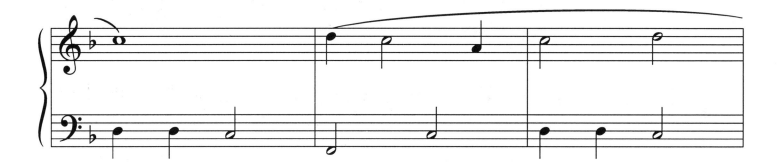

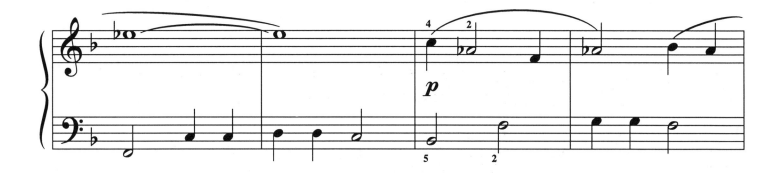

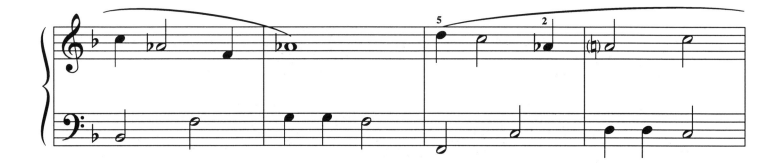

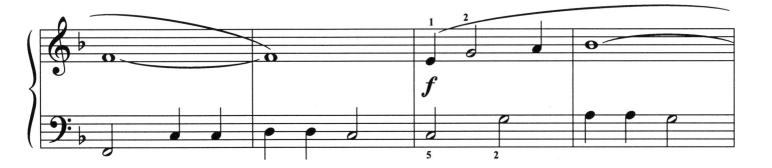

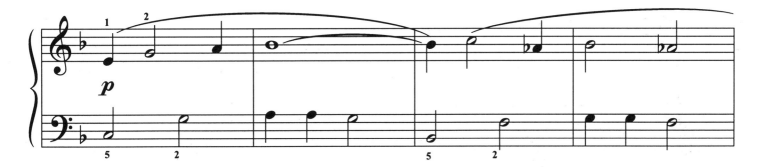

Empty Pocket Blues

Wesley Schaum

Allegretto ♩= 92-104

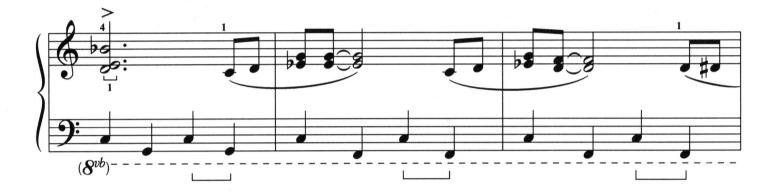

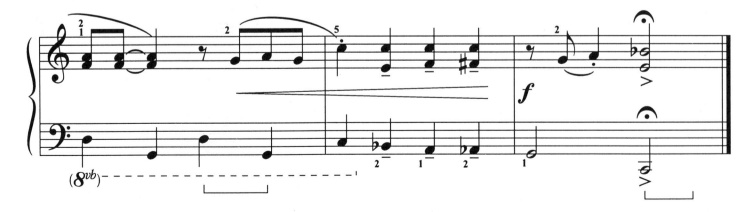

If desired, Swing 8th notes may be used: 🎵 = 🎵

High Energy

Wesley Schaum

Super Boogie

Wesley Schaum

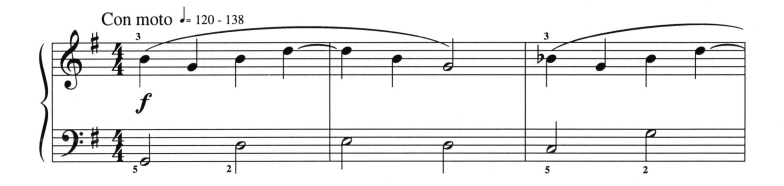

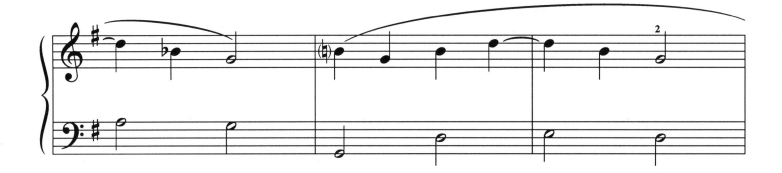

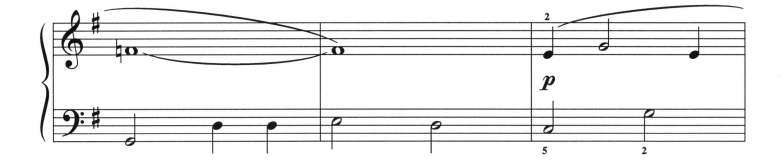

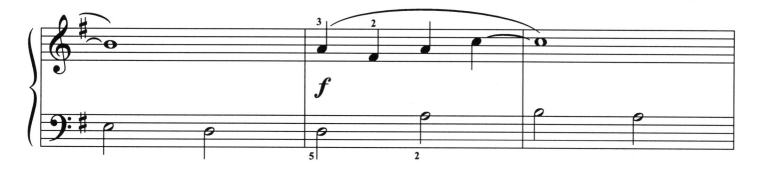

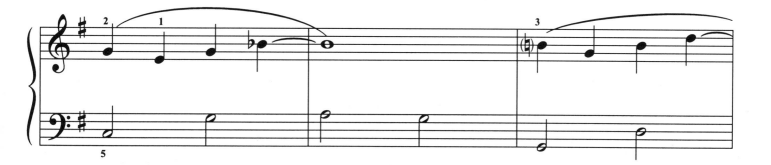

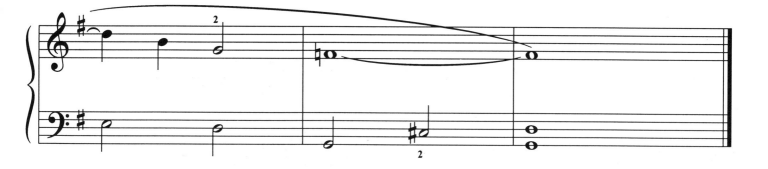

Solid Stomp

Wesley Schaum

Bubble Boogie

Wesley Schaum

L.H. one octave lower throughout.

If desired, Swing 8th notes may be used: